THE

*Note*BIBLE

PART BIBLE, PART NOTEBOOK

SELECT EDITION
New Testament Colossians

LARGE PRINT
FIRST EDITION

This NoteBible belongs to

Check out all of our editions of the NoteBible!
VISIT WWW.NOTEBIBLE.COM

THE NOTEBIBLE: Select Edition - New Testament Colossians
First Edition

The World English Bible is a work in the public domain.
The NoteBible product design and assembly are products of
Scroll Media.

ISBN-13: 978-0692550021 (Scroll Media)
ISBN-10: 069255002X

The NoteBible
www.notebible.com

Scroll Media Company
www.scrollmedia.com

Scroll Bookstore
www.scrollbookstore.com

Printed in the United States of America.

Contents

Dedication

To Humanity,

From the Father,
Jesus Christ of Nazareth,
Holy Spirit

Preface
to the World English Bible

What is the Holy Bible?

The Holy Bible is a collection of books and letters written by many people who were inspired by the Holy Spirit of God. These books tell us how we can be saved from the evil of this world and gain eternal life that is truly worth living. Although the Holy Bible contains rules of conduct, it is not just a rule book. It reveals God's heart—a Father's heart, full of love and compassion. The Holy Bible tells you what you need to know and believe to be saved from sin and evil and how to live a life that is truly worth living, no matter what your current circumstances may be.

The Holy Bible consists of two main sections: the Old Testament (including Psalms and Proverbs) and the New Testament (Matthew through Revelation). The Old Testament records God's interaction with mankind before He sent His son to redeem us, while recording prophesy predicting that coming. The New Testament tells us of God's Son and Anointed One, Jesus, and the wonderful salvation that He purchased for us.

The same Holy Spirit who inspired the Holy Bible is living among us today, and He is happy to help you understand what He intended as you study His Word. Just ask Him, and He is more than happy to help you apply His message to your life.

The Old Testament was originally written mostly in Hebrew. The New Testament was originally written mostly in the common street Greek (not the formal Greek used for official legal matters). The Holy Bible is translated into many languages, and being translated into many more, so that everyone may have an opportunity to hear the Good News about Jesus Christ.

Why was the World English Bible

translated?

There are already many good translations of the Holy Bible into contemporary English. Unfortunately, almost all of them are restricted by copyright and copyright holder policy. This restricts publication and republication of God's Word in many ways, such as in downloadable files on the Internet, use of extensive quotations in books, etc. The World English Bible was commissioned by God in response to prayer about this subject.

Because the World English Bible is in the Public Domain (not copyrighted), it can be freely copied, distributed, and redistributed without any payment of royalties. You don't even have to ask permission to do so. You may publish the whole World English Bible in book form, bind it in leather and sell it. You may incorporate it into your Bible study software.

You may make and distribute audio recordings of it. You may broadcast it. All you have to do is maintain the integrity of God's Word before God, and reserve the name "World English Bible" for faithful copies of this translation.

How was the World English Bible translated?

The World English Bible is an update of the American Standard Version (ASV) of the Holy Bible, published in 1901. A custom computer program updated the archaic words and word forms to contemporary equivalents, and then a team of volunteers proofread and updated the grammar. The New Testament was updated to conform to the Majority Text reconstruction of the original Greek manuscripts, thus taking advantage of the superior access to manuscripts that we have now compared to when the original ASV was translated.

What is different about the World English Bible?

The style of the World English Bible, while fairly literally translated, is in informal, spoken English. The World English Bible is designed to sound good and be accurate when read aloud. It is not formal in its language, just as the original Greek of the New Testament was not formal. The WEB uses contractions rather freely.

The World English Bible doesn't capitalize pronouns pertaining to God. The original manuscripts made no such distinction. Hebrew has no such thing as upper and lower case, and the original Greek manuscripts were written in all upper case letters. Attempting to add in such a distinction raises some difficulties in translating dual-meaning Scriptures such as the coronation psalms.

The World English Bible main edition translates God's Proper Name in the Old Testament as "Yahweh." The Messianic Edition and the British Edition of the World English Bible translates the same name as "LORD" (all capital letters), or when used with "Lord" (mixed case, translated from "Adonai",) GOD. There are solid translational arguments for both traditions.

Because World English Bible uses the Majority Text as the basis for the New Testament, you may notice the following differences in comparing the WEB to other translations:

The order of Matthew 23:13 and 14 is reversed in some translations.

Luke 17:36 and Acts 15:34, which are not found in the majority of the Greek Manuscripts (and are relegated to footnotes in the WEB) may be included in some other translations.

Romans 14:24-26 in the WEB may appear as Romans 16:25-27 in other translations.

1 John 5:7-8 contains an addition in some translations, including the KJV. Erasmus admitted adding this text to his published Greek New Testament, even though he could at first find no Greek manuscript support for it, because he was being pressured by men to do so, and because he didn't see any doctrinal harm in it. Lots of things not written by John in this letter are true, but we decline to add them to what the Holy Spirit inspired through John.

With all of the above and some other places where lack of clarity in the original manuscripts has led to multiple possible readings, significant variants are listed in footnotes. The reading that in our prayerful judgment is best is in the main text. Overall, the World English

Bible doesn't differ very much from several other good contemporary English translations of the Holy Bible. The message of Salvation through Jesus Christ is still the same. The point of this translation was not to be very different (except for legal status), but to update the ASV for readability while retaining or improving the accuracy of that well-respected translation and retaining the public domain status of the ASV.

Does the World English Bible include the Apocrypha?

The World English Bible is an ecumenical project that includes books included in Bibles in many denominations. The main 66 books of the Old and New Testaments are recognized as Scripture by all true Christians. There are also books considered to be part of, depending on which book and who you ask, Deuterocanon, Apocrypha, and Pseudepigrapha.

The following books and parts of books are recognized as Deuterocanonical Scripture by the Roman Catholic, Greek, and Russian Orthodox Churches: Tobit, Judith, Esther from the Greek Septuagint, The Wisdom of Solomon, Ecclesiasticus (also called The Wisdom of Jesus Son of Sirach), Baruch, The Song of the Three Holy Children, Susanna, and Bel and the Dragon, 1 Maccabees, 2 Maccabees. In this edition, The Letter of Jeremiah is included as chapter 6 of Baruch. Three of those books come from parts of Daniel found in the Greek Septuagint, but not the Hebrew Old Testament: The Song of the Three Holy Children, Susanna, and Bel and the Dragon. These 11 books, plus the 66 books of the Old and New Testaments comprise the 88 books in the

Roman Catholic Bible.

The following books are recognized as Deuterocanonical Scripture by the Greek and Russian Orthodox Churches, but not the Roman Catholic Church: 1 Esdras, The Prayer of Manasseh, Psalm 151, and 3 Maccabees. Note that 1 Esdras and the Prayer of Manasseh are also in an appendix to the Latin Vulgate Bible.

The Slavonic Bible includes 2 Esdras, but calls it 3 Esdras. This same book is in the Appendix to the Latin Vulgate as 4 Esdras.

An appendix to the Greek Septuagint contains 4 Maccabees. It is included for its historical value.

Among Christian denominations and among individual Christians, opinions vary widely on the Deuterocanon/Apocrypha, as do the collective names they give them. Many regard them as useful in gaining additional understanding of the Old and New Testaments and the hand of God in history, even if they don't give them the same status as the 66 books of the Old and New Testaments. They are included here in support of the churches and individuals who read them and use them, as separate from, but frequently used with, the core canon of the 66 books of the Holy Bible.

What are MT, TR, and NU?

In the footnotes, MT refers to the Greek Majority Text New Testament, which is the authoritative basis for this translation. TR stands for Textus Receptus, which is the Greek Text from which the King James Version New Testament was translated. NU stands for the Nestle-Aland/UBS critical text of the Greek New Testament, which is used as a basis for some other Bible translations.

More Information

For answers to frequently asked questions about the World English Bible, please visit WorldEnglishBible.org.

Editor's Note: All prefaces from the World English Bible are the same in all NoteBibles so readers understand why the NoteBible is available in these editions.

SCROLL
MEDIA

From
Scroll Media

Welcome to the NoteBible, a tool we hope can make it easier for people wanting to dig deep into the Word of God to keep and maintain important notes they make about how God speaks to them through scripture.

We do not claim this translation of the Bible. It is a blessing to be in the public domain and available for us to turn into this note-takers tool.

Because this book is about digging into the Word, we encourage you not to fear being dainty. This is a workbook, meant to be worked. While the Word of

God is holy, the paper and ink are not, so if you find a particular favorite verse and wish to keep it as near your heart as possible, and feel you must rip it out of this book and fold it into your shirt or back pocket, do so!

Do whatever it takes to engage with and bury deep in your soul the Word of the Living God.

We wish you the very best in your pursuit of a better relationship with Christ, and hope this remains just another, effective tool in your journey to that life.

As to the percentage of direct accuracy of the World English Bible to the original texts, in comparison to, say, the English Standard, New King James, New American Standard or some other version, we cannot say.

Without your own personal study of the spoken and written languages in which the Bible was embued, or a deep inspection of the cultures from which these languages sprung, no "modern" version will give you the most accurate translation.

Too many inside jokes, colloquialisms and high-context cultural references fill the Bible across multiple cultures to adequately describe it accurately 100 percent within the pages of any translation, however thorough.

Therefore, we recommend using more than one version in your study. Use the NoteBible to capture your thoughts, but contrast with other editions and let each translator's attempt to describe the original give you a well-rounded understand, for no one can give you a perfect vocal description of any painting as well as merely opening your eyes to it, yourself.

So, all the best to you in your study of His Word. Thank you and God bless!

For your
Study

There is no perfect way to study the Bible, because there is no perfect way to understand the Word of God outside a living relationship with Jesus Christ. While many theories exist as to the best method of study, historical analysis and understanding of the Word (evidenced by the many denominations of Christian faith which have sprung up over the centuries), the final authority on understanding scripture comes from God, Himself.

The best way to get that? A regular intake and study of the scriptures, meditation upon them, and quieting yourself before God so that He may reveal to you the true meaning of His words.

This isn't to say you shouldn't learn from others who have gone before you. Not everyone would care to learn Greek, Hebrew, Aramaic and Latin, but if you study the writings of those who have, you expand your understanding of the culture, language and intent of the scribes of this fantastic volume known as the Bible.

While there is no perfect way to study, it is wise to start with simple, poignant questions that anyone can ask in the privacy of their own quiet time, or in a group study session, to help them dig deeper with God and His Word.

This the **Sharrow Quadrant Method**. When you reach a verse or passage that stands out to you, or one in which you feel God is instructing you to seek out, directly, pose these questions to yourself silently or by answering them on a sheet of loose paper.

Humanity

What does this verse/passage tell me about myself? The human condition? Significant facts about history and the culture in which the verse is set?

Respond

How do I live in response to this reading? How will my walk with God *this week* be different by application? How does His Word change me?

God

What does this verse/passage tell me about God? His observed character, personality, desires, behaviors, who He is and how He operates?

Define

What does the verse mean? What don't I understand? Is it weird to me? Why? Does it make me feel inspired or unsettled? What's important about it?

This method was developed by Mike Sharrow, San Antonio, Texas.

Paul's Letter to the

Colossians

Favorite Verses? Important points? Thoughts?

_____

_____

_____

_____

_____

_____

_____

_____

_____

1

1 Paul, an apostle of Christ Jesus through the will of God, and Timothy our brother, 2 to the saints and faithful brothers in Christ at Colossae: Grace to you and peace from God our Father, and the Lord Jesus Christ.

3 We give thanks to God the Father of our Lord Jesus Christ, praying always for you, 4 having heard of your faith in Christ Jesus, and of the love which you have toward all the saints, 5 because of the hope which is laid up for you in the heavens, of which you heard before in the word of the truth of the Good News, 6 which has come to you; even as it is in all the world and is bearing fruit

and growing, as it does in you also, since the day you heard and knew the grace of God in truth; 7 even as you learned of Epaphras our beloved fellow servant, who is a faithful servant of Christ on your behalf, 8 who also declared to us your love in the Spirit.

9 For this cause, we also, since the day we heard this, don't cease praying and making requests for you, that you may be filled with the knowledge of his will in all spiritual wisdom and understanding, 10 that you may walk worthily of the Lord, to please him in all respects, bearing fruit in every good work, and increasing in the knowledge of God; 11 strengthened with

all power, according to the might of his glory, for all endurance and perseverance with joy; 12 giving thanks to the Father, who made us fit to be partakers of the inheritance of the saints in light; 13 who delivered us out of the power of darkness, and translated us into the Kingdom of the Son of his love; 14 in whom we have our redemption, the forgiveness of our sins; 15 who is the image of the invisible God, the firstborn of all creation. 16 For by him all things were created, in the heavens and on the earth, things visible and things invisible, whether thrones or dominions or principalities or powers; all things have been created through him, and for him. 17 He is before all things, and in him all things are held together. 18 He is the head of the body, the assembly, who is the beginning, the firstborn from the dead; that in all things he might have the preeminence. 19 For all the fullness was pleased to dwell in him; 20 and through him to reconcile all things to himself, by him, whether things on the earth, or things in the heavens, having made peace through the blood of his cross.

21 You, being in past times alienated and enemies in your mind in your evil deeds, 22 yet now he has reconciled in the body of his flesh through death, to present you holy and without defect and blameless

before him, 23 if it is
so that you continue
in the faith, grounded
and steadfast, and
not moved away
from the hope of the
Good News which
you heard, which is
being proclaimed in all
creation under heaven;
of which I, Paul, was
made a servant.

24 Now I rejoice
in my sufferings for
your sake, and fill
up on my part that
which is lacking of the
afflictions of Christ
in my flesh for his
body's sake, which
is the assembly; 25 of
which I was made a
servant, according to
the stewardship of
God which was given
me toward you, to
fulfill the word of God,
26 the mystery which
has been hidden for
ages and generations.
But now it has been

revealed to his saints, 27 to whom God was pleased to make known what are the riches of the glory of this mystery among the Gentiles, which is Christ in you, the hope of glory; 28 whom we proclaim, admonishing every man and teaching every man in all wisdom, that we may present every man perfect in Christ Jesus; 29 for which I also labor, striving according to his working, which works in me mightily.

2

1 For I desire to have you know how greatly I struggle for you, and for those at Laodicea, and for as many as have not seen my face in the flesh; 2 that their hearts may be comforted, they being knit

together in love, and gaining all riches of the full assurance of understanding, that they may know the mystery of God, both of the Father and of Christ, 3 in whom are all the treasures of wisdom and knowledge hidden. 4 Now this I say that no one may delude you with persuasiveness of speech. 5 For though I am absent in the flesh, yet am I with you in the spirit, rejoicing and seeing your order, and the steadfastness of your faith in Christ.

6 As therefore you received Christ Jesus, the Lord, walk in him, 7 rooted and built up in him, and established in the faith, even as you were taught, abounding in it in thanksgiving.

8 Be careful that

you don't let anyone rob you through his philosophy and vain deceit, after the tradition of men, after the elements of the world, and not after Christ. 9 For in him all the fullness of the Deity dwells bodily, 10 and in him you are made full, who is the head of all principality and power; 11 in whom you were also circumcised with a circumcision not made with hands, in the putting off of the body of the sins of the flesh, in the circumcision of Christ; 12 having been buried with him in baptism, in which you were also raised with him through faith in the working of God, who raised him from the dead. 13 You were dead through your trespasses and the uncircumcision of your flesh. He made you alive together with him, having forgiven us all our trespasses, 14 wiping out the handwriting in ordinances which was against us; and he has taken it out of the way, nailing it to the cross; 15 having stripped the principalities and the powers, he made a show of them openly, triumphing over them in it.

16 Let no one therefore judge you in eating, or in drinking, or with respect to a feast day or a new moon or a Sabbath day, 17 which are a shadow of the things to come; but the body is Christ's. 18 Let no one rob you of your prize by a voluntary humility and worshiping of the

angels, dwelling in the things which he has not seen, vainly puffed up by his fleshly mind, 19 and not holding firmly to the Head, from whom all the body, being supplied and knit together through the joints and ligaments, grows with God's growth.

20 If you died with Christ from the elements of the world, why, as though living in the world, do you subject yourselves to ordinances, 21 "Don't handle, nor taste, nor touch" 22 (all of which perish with use), according to the precepts and doctrines of men? 23 Which things indeed appear like wisdom in self-imposed worship, and humility, and severity to the body; but aren't of any value against

the indulgence of the flesh.

3

1 If then you were raised together with Christ, seek the things that are above, where Christ is, seated on the right hand of God. 2 Set your mind on the things that are above, not on the things that are on the earth. 3 For you died, and your life is hidden with Christ in God. 4 When Christ, our life, is revealed, then you will also be revealed with him in glory.

5 Put to death therefore your members which are on the earth: sexual immorality, uncleanness, depraved passion, evil desire, and covetousness, which is idolatry; 6 for which things' sake the wrath of God comes

on the children of disobedience. 7 You also once walked in those, when you lived in them; 8 but now you also put them all away: anger, wrath, malice, slander, and shameful speaking out of your mouth. 9 Don't lie to one another, seeing that you have put off the old man with his doings, 10 and have put on the new man, who is being renewed in knowledge after the image of his Creator, 11 where there can't be Greek and Jew, circumcision and uncircumcision, barbarian, Scythian, bondservant, freeman; but Christ is all, and in all.

12 Put on therefore, as God's chosen ones, holy and beloved, a heart of compassion, kindness,

lowliness, humility, and perseverance; 13 bearing with one another, and forgiving each other, if any man has a complaint against any; even as Christ forgave you, so you also do.

14 Above all these things, walk in love, which is the bond of perfection. 15 And let the peace of God rule in your hearts, to which also you were called in one body; and be thankful. 16 Let the word of Christ dwell in you richly; in all wisdom teaching and admonishing one another with psalms, hymns, and spiritual songs, singing with grace in your heart to the Lord.

17 Whatever you do, in word or in deed, do all in the name of the Lord Jesus, giving

thanks to God the Father, through him.

18 Wives, be in subjection to your husbands, as is fitting in the Lord.

19 Husbands, love your wives, and don't be bitter against them.

20 Children, obey your parents in all things, for this pleases the Lord.

21 Fathers, don't provoke your children, so that they won't be discouraged.

22 Servants, obey in all things those who are your masters according to the flesh, not just when they are looking, as men pleasers, but in singleness of heart, fearing God. 23 And whatever you do, work heartily, as for the Lord, and not for men, 24 knowing that from the Lord you will

receive the reward
of the inheritance;
for you serve the
Lord Christ. 25 But
he who does wrong
will receive again for
the wrong that he has
done, and there is no
partiality.

4

1 Masters, give to
your servants that
which is just and
equal, knowing that
you also have a Master
in heaven.

2 Continue
steadfastly in prayer,
watching therein with
thanksgiving; 3 praying
together for us also,
that God may open to
us a door for the word,
to speak the mystery
of Christ, for which
I am also in bonds;
4 that I may reveal it
as I ought to speak.
5 Walk in wisdom
toward those who are
outside, redeeming the

time. 6 Let your speech always be with grace, seasoned with salt, that you may know how you ought to answer each one.

7 All my affairs will be made known to you by Tychicus, the beloved brother, faithful servant, and fellow bondservant in the Lord. 8 I am sending him to you for this very purpose, that he may know your circumstances and comfort your hearts, 9 together with Onesimus, the faithful and beloved brother, who is one of you. They will make known to you everything that is going on here.

10 Aristarchus, my fellow prisoner, greets you, and Mark, the cousin of Barnabas (concerning whom you received

commandments, "if he comes to you, receive him"), 11 and Jesus who is called Justus. These are my only fellow workers for God's Kingdom who are of the circumcision, men who have been a comfort to me.

12 Epaphras, who is one of you, a servant of Christ, salutes you, always striving for you in his prayers, that you may stand perfect and complete in all the will of God. 13 For I testify about him, that he has great zeal for you, and for those in Laodicea, and for those in Hierapolis. 14 Luke, the beloved physician, and Demas greet you. 15 Greet the brothers who are in Laodicea, and Nymphas, and the assembly that is in his house. 16 When this

letter has been read among you, cause it to be read also in the assembly of the Laodiceans; and that you also read the letter from Laodicea. 17 Tell Archippus, "Take heed to the ministry which you have received in the Lord, that you fulfill it."

18 The salutation of me, Paul, with my own hand: remember my bonds. Grace be with you. Amen.

COLOSSIANS

COLOSSIANS

Glossary

The following words used in the World English Bible (WEB) are not very common, either because they refer to ancient weights, measures, or money, or because they are in some way unique to the Bible. If you find words in the World English Bible that you think should be added to this list, or if you have comments or corrections for this list, please let us know.

Abaddon

Abaddon is Hebrew for destruction.

Abba

Abba is a Chaldee word for father, used in a respectful, affectionate, and familiar way, like papa, dad, or daddy. Often used in prayer to refer to our Father in Heaven.

adultery

Adultery is having sexual intercourse with someone besides your own husband or wife. In the Bible, the only legitimate sexual intercourse is between a man and a woman who are married to each other.

alpha

Alpha is the first letter of the Greek alphabet. It is sometimes used to mean the beginning or the first.

amen

Amen means "So be it" or "I believe it is certainly so."

angel

"Angel" literally means "messenger" or "envoy," and is usually used to refer to spiritual beings who normally are invisible to us, but can also appear as exceedingly strong creatures or as humans.

Apollyon

Apollyon is Greek for destroyer.

apostle

"Apostle" means a delegate, messenger, or one sent forth with orders. This term is applied in the New Testament in both a general sense connected with a ministry

of establishing and strengthening church fellowships, as well as in a specific sense to "The 12 Apostles of the Lamb" (Revelation 21:14). The former category applies to a specific ministry that continues in the Church (Ephesians 4:11-13) and which includes many more than 12 people, while the latter refers to the apostles named in Matthew 10:2-4, except with Judas Iscariot replaced by Matthias (Acts 1:26).

Armageddon

See Har-magedon.

assarion

An assarion is a small Roman copper coin worth one tenth of a drachma, or about an hour's wages for an agricultural laborer.

aureus

An aureus is a Roman gold coin, worth 25 silver denarii. An aureus weighed from 115 to 126.3 grains

(7.45 to 8.18 grams).

baptize

Baptize means to immerse in, or wash with something, usually water. Baptism in the Holy Spirit, fire, the Body of Christ, and suffering are also mentioned in the New Testament, along with baptism in water. Baptism is not just to cleanse the body, but as an outward sign of an inward spiritual cleansing and commitment. Baptism is a sign of repentance, as practiced by John the Baptizer, and of faith in Jesus Christ, as practiced by Jesus' disciples.

bath

A bath is a liquid measure of about 22 liters, 5.8 U. S. gallons, or 4.8 imperial gallons.

batos

A batos is a liquid measure of about 39.5 liters, 10.4 U. S. gallons, or 8.7 imperial gallons.

Beelzebul

literally, lord of the flies. A name used for the devil.

Beersheba

Beersheba is Hebrew for "well of the oath" or "well of the seven." A city in Israel.

behold

Look! See! Wow! Notice this! Lo!

cherub

A cherub is a kind of angel with wings and hands that is associated with the throne room of God and guardian duty. See Ezekiel 10.

cherubim

Cherubim means more than one cherub or a mighty cherub.

choenix

A choenix is a dry volume measure that is a little more than a liter (which is a little more than a quart). A choenix was the daily ration of grain for a soldier in some armies.

concubine

a woman who is united to a man for the purpose of providing him with sexual pleasure and children, but not being honored as a full partner in marriage; a second-class wife. In Old Testament times (and in some places now), it was the custom of middle-eastern kings, chiefs, and wealthy men to marry multiple wives and concubines, but God commanded the Kings of Israel not to do so (Deuteronomy 17:17) and Jesus encouraged people to either remain single or marry as God originally intended: one man married to one woman (Matthew 19:3-12; 1 Corinthians 7:1-13).

cor

A cor is a dry measure of about 391 liters, 103 U. S. gallons, or 86 imperial gallons.

corban

Corban is a Hebrew word for an offering devoted to God.

crucify

Crucify means to execute someone by nailing them to a cross with metal spikes. Their hands are stretched out on the crossbeam with spikes driven through their wrists or hands. Their feet or ankles are attached to a cross with a metal spike. The weight of the victim's body tends to force the air out of his lungs. To rise up to breathe, the victim has to put weight on the wounds, and use a lot of strength. The victim is nailed to the cross while the cross is on the ground, then the cross is raised up and dropped into a hole, thus jarring the wounds. Before crucifixion, the victim was usually whipped with a

Roman cat of nine tails, which had bits of glass and metal tied to its ends. This caused chunks of flesh to be removed and open wounds to be placed against the raw wood of the cross. The victim was made to carry the heavy crossbeam of his cross from the place of judgment to the place of crucifixion, but often was physically unable after the scourging, so another person would be pressed into involuntary service to carry the cross for him. Roman crucifixion was generally done totally naked to maximize both shame and discomfort. Eventually, the pain, weakness, dehydration, and exhaustion of the muscles needed to breathe make breathing impossible, and the victim suffocates.

cubit

A cubit is a unit of linear measure, from the elbow to the tip of the longest finger of a man. This unit is commonly converted to 0.46 meters or 18 inches, although that varies with height of the man doing the measurement. There is also a "long" cubit that is longer than a regular cubit by a handbreadth. (Ezekiel 43:13)

cummin

Cummin is an aromatic seed from Cuminum cyminum, resembling caraway in flavor and appearance. It is used as a spice.

darnel

Darnel is a weed grass (probably bearded darnel or Lolium temulentum) that looks very much like wheat until it is mature, when the seeds reveal a great difference. Darnel seeds aren't good for much except as chicken feed or to burn to prevent the spread of this weed.

denarii

denarii: plural form of denarius, a silver Roman coin worth about a day's wages for a laborer.

denarius

A denarius is a silver Roman coin worth about a day's wages for an agricultural laborer. A denarius was worth 1/25th of a Roman aureus.

devil

The word "devil" comes from the Greek "diabolos," which means "one prone to slander; a liar." "Devil" is used to refer to a fallen angel, also called "Satan," who works to steal, kill, destroy, and do evil. The devil's doom is certain, and it is only a matter of time before he is thrown into the Lake of Fire, never to escape.

didrachma

A didrachma is a Greek silver coin worth 2 drachmas, about as much as 2 Roman denarii, or about 2 days wages. It was commonly used to pay the half-shekel temple tax.

distaff

part of a spinning wheel used for twisting threads.

drachma

A drachma is a Greek silver coin worth about one Roman denarius, or about a day's wages for an agricultural laborer.
El-Elohe-Israel
El-Elohe-Israel means "God, the God of Israel" or "The God of Israel is mighty."

ephah

An ephah is a measure of volume of about 22 liters, 5.8 U. S. gallons, 4.8 imperial gallons, or a bit more than half a bushel.

Gehenna

Gehenna is one word used for Hell. It comes from the Hebrew Gey-Hinnom, literally "valley of Hinnom." This word originated as the name for a place south of the old city of Jerusalem where the city's rubbish was burned. At one time, live babies were thrown crying into the fire under the arms of the idol, Moloch, to die there. This place was so despised by the people after the righteous King Josiah abolished this hideous practice that it was made into a garbage heap. Bodies of diseased animals and executed criminals were thrown there and burned.

gittith

Gittith is a musical term possibly meaning "an instrument of Gath."

goad

a sharp, pointed prodding device used to motivate reluctant animals (such as oxen and mules) to move in the right direction.

gospel

Gospel means "good news" or "glad tidings," specifically the Good News of Jesus' life, death, and resurrection for our salvation, healing, and provision; and the hope of eternal life that Jesus made available to us by God's grace.

Hades

Hades: The nether realm of the disembodied spirits. Also known as "hell." See also "Sheol".

Har-magedon

Har-magedon, also called Armegeddon, is most likely a reference to hill ("har") of Megiddo, near the Carmel Range in Israel. This area has a large valley plain with plenty of room for armies to maneuver.

hin

A hin was about 6.5 liters or 1.7 gallons.

homer

One homer is about 220 liters, 6.2 U. S. bushels,

6.1 imperial bushels, 58 U. S. gallons, or 48.4 imperial gallons.

hypocrite

a stage actor; someone who pretends to be someone other than who they really are; a pretender; a dissembler

Ishmael

Ishmael is the son of Abraham and Hagar. Ishmael literally means, "God hears."

Jehovah

See "Yahweh."

Jesus

"Jesus" is Greek for the Hebrew name "Yeshua," which is a short version of "Yehoshua," which comes from "Yoshia," which means "He will save."

kodrantes

A kodrantes is a small coin worth one half of an Attic chalcus or two lepta. It is worth less than 2% of a day's wages for an agricultural laborer.

lepta

Lepta are very small, brass, Jewish coins worth half a Roman quadrans each, which is worth a quarter of the copper assarion. Lepta are worth less than 1% of an agricultural worker's daily wages.

leviathan

Leviathan is a poetic name for a large aquatic creature, posssibly a crocodile or a dinosaur.

mahalath

Mahalath is the name of a tune or a musical term.

manna

Name for the food that God miraculously provided to the Israelites while they were wandering in the wilderness between Egypt and the promised land. From Hebrew man-hu (What is that?) or manan (to allot). See Exodus 16:14-35.

marriage

the union of a husband and

a wife for the purpose of cohabitation, procreation, and to enjoy each other's company. God's plan for marriage is between one man and one woman (Mark 10:6-9; 1 Corinthians 7). Although there are many cases of a man marrying more than one woman in the Old Testament, being married to one wife is a requirement to serve in certain church leadership positions (1 Timothy 3:2,12; Titus 1:5-6).

maschil

Maschil is a musical and literary term for "contemplation" or "meditative psalm."

michtam

A michtam is a poem.

mina

A mina is a Greek coin worth 100 Greek drachmas (or 100 Roman denarii), or about 100 day's wages for an agricultural laborer.

myrrh

Myrrh is the fragrant substance that oozes out of the stems and branches of the low, shrubby tree commiphora myrrha or comiphora kataf native to the Arabian deserts and parts of Africa. The fragrant gum drops to the ground and hardens into an oily yellowish-brown resin. Myrrh was highly valued as a perfume, and as an ingredient in medicinal and ceremonial ointments.

Nicolaitans

Nicolaitans were most likely Gnostics who taught the detestable lie that the physical and spiritual realms were entirely separate and that immorality in the physical realm wouldn't harm your spiritual health.

omega

Omega is the last letter of the Greek alphabet. It is sometimes used to mean the last or the end.

Peniel

Peniel is Hebrew for "face of God."

phylactery

a leather container for holding a small scroll containing important Scripture passages that is worn on the arm or forehead in prayer. These phylacteries (tefillin in Hebrew) are still used by orthodox Jewish men. See Deuteronomy 6:8.

Praetorium

Praetorium: the Roman governor's residence and office building, and those who work there.

quadrans

A quadrans is a Roman coin worth about 1/64 of a denarius. A denarius is about one day's wages for an agricultural laborer.

rabbi

Rabbi is a transliteration of the Hebrew word for "my teacher," used as a title of respect for Jewish teachers.

Rahab

Rahab is either (1) The prostitute who hid Joshua's 2 spies in Jericho (Joshua 2,6) and later became an ancestor of Jesus (Matthew 1:5) and an example of faith (Hebrews 11:31; James 2:25); or (2) Literally, "pride" or "arrogance" — possibly a reference to a large aquatic creature (Job 9:13; 26:12; Isaiah 51:9) or symbolically referring to Egypt (Psalm 87:4; 89:10; Isaiah 30:7).

repent

to change one's mind; turn away from sin and turn towards God; to abhor one's past sins and determine to follow God.

Rhabboni

Rhabboni: a transliteration of the Hebrew word for "great teacher."

Sabbath

The seventh day of the

week, set aside by God for man to rest.

saints

The Greek word for "saints" literally means "holy ones." Saints are people set apart for service to God as holy and separate, living in righteousness. Used in the Bible to refer to all Christians and to all of those who worship Yahweh in Old Testament times.

Samaritan

A Samaritan is a resident of Samaria. The Samaritans and the Jews generally detested each other during the time that Jesus walked among us.

sanctify

To declare or set apart something as holy. To purify and separate a person from sin.

sata

A sata is a dry measure of capacity approximately equal to 13 liters or 1.5 pecks.

Satan

Satan means "accuser." This is one name for the devil, an enemy of God and God's people.

scribe

A scribe is one who copies God's law. They were often respected as teachers and authorities on God's law.

selah

Selah is a musical term indicating a pause or instrumental interlude for reflection.

seraphim

Seraphim are 6-winged angels. See Isaiah 6:2-6.

sexual immorality

The term "sexual immorality" in the New Testament comes from the Greek "porneia," which refers to any sexual activity besides that between a husband and his wife. In other words, prostitution (male or female), bestiality, homosexual activity, any sexual intercourse outside of marriage, and the production and consumption of pornography all are included in this term.

shekel
A measure of weight, and when referring to that weight in gold, silver, or brass, of money. A shekel is approximately 16 grams, about a half an ounce, or 20 gerahs (Ezekiel 45:12).

Sheol
Sheol is the place of the dead. See also "Hades".

Shibah
Shibah is Hebrew for "oath" or "seven." See Beersheba.

shigionoth
Victorious music.

soul
"Soul" refers to the emotions and intellect of a living person, as well as that person's very life. It is distinguished in the Bible from a person's spirit and body. (1 Thessalonians 5:23, Hebrews 4:12)

span
A span is the length from the tip of a man's thumb to the tip of his little finger when his hand is stretched out (about half a cubit, or 9 inches, or 22.8 cm.)

spirit
Spirit, breath, and wind all derive from the same Hebrew and Greek words. A person's spirit is the very essence of that person's life, which comes from God, who is a Spirit being (John 4:24, Genesis 1:2; 2:7). The Bible distinguishes between a person's spirit, soul, and body (1 Thessalonians 5:23, Hebrews 4:12). Some beings may exist as spirits without necessarily having a visible body, such as angels and demons (Luke 9:39, 1 John 4:1-3).

stadia

Stadia is plural for "stadion," a linear measure of about 184.9 meters or 606.6 feet (the length of the race course at Olympia).

stater

A stater is a Greek silver coin equivalent to four Attic or two Alexandrian drachmas, or a Jewish shekel: just exactly enough to cover the half-shekel Temple Tax for two people.

tabernacle

a dwelling place or place of worship, usually a tent.

talent

A measure of weight or mass of 3000 shekels.

Tartarus

Tartarus is the Greek name for an underworld for the wicked dead; another name for Gehenna or Hell.

teraphim

Teraphim are household idols that may have been associated with inheritance rights to the household property.

Yah

"Yah" is a shortened form of "Yahweh," which is God's proper name. This form is used occasionally in the Old Testament, mostly in the Psalms. See "Yahweh."

Yahweh

"Yahweh" is God's proper name. In Hebrew, the four consonants roughly equivalent to YHWH were considered too holy to pronounce, so the Hebrew word for "Lord" (Adonai) was substituted when reading it aloud. When vowel points were added to the Hebrew Old Testament, the vowel points for "Adonai" were mixed with the consonants for "Yahweh," which if you pronounced it literally as written, would be pronounced "Yehovah" or "Jehovah." When the Old Testament was translated to Greek, the tradition of substituting "Lord" for God's proper name continued in the translation of God's name to "Lord" (Kurios). Some English Bibles translate God's proper name to "LORD" or "GOD" (usually with small capital letters), based on that same tradition. This can get really confusing, since two other words ("Adonai" and "Elohim") translate to "Lord" and "God," and they are sometimes used together. The ASV of 1901 (and some other translations) render YHWH as "Jehovah." The most probable pronunciation of God's proper name is "Yahweh." In Hebrew, the name "Yahweh" is related to the active declaration "I AM." See Exodus 3:13-14. Since Hebrew has no tenses, the declaration "I AM" can also be interpreted as "I WAS" and "I WILL BE." Compare Revelation 1:8.

Zion

Zion is a name which originally referred one of the mountains of Jerusalem. It became a term synonymous with Jerusalem itself. The term "Heavenly Zion" is also used to refer the future dwelling place of God's people.

More from Scroll Media

THE *Note*BIBLE

FULL TESTAMENTS
NonCore Compendium
New Testament

TRADITIONAL GROUPS
The Law
OT History
Poetry
Major Prophets
Minor Prophets
Gospels
NT History
Paul's Letters to Churches
Paul's Letters to Friends
General Letters

SELECT EDITIONS
Psalms
Proverbs & Ecclesiastes
Luke
Romans
Colossians
Daniel & Revelation

SPECIAL EDITIONS
Workbooks
The Gospels (Red Letter)
The Story of David
The Story of Jesus
The Sayings of Jesus
Prophecy of Revelation

MORE INFORMATION

To download a free ebook, Kindle or audiobook of the World English Bible, visit www.NoteBible.com or www. WorldEnglishBible.org.

Explore all our resources at NoteBible.com, or visit the links below to see what else Scroll Media offers.

www.ScrollBookStore.com / www.ScrollMedia.com

www.ingramcontent.com/pod-product-compliance
Lightning Source LLC
Chambersburg PA
CBHW060539030426
42337CB00021B/4338